MEL BAY PRESENTS

POCKE   OK DELUXE SERIES
by William Bay

1 2 3 4 5 6 7 8 9 0

Table of Contents

3

Diatonic Harmonica

↑ = BLOW   ↓ = DRAW

| 1 | 2 | 3 | 4 | 5 | 6 | 7 | 8 | 9 | 10 |

How to Read the Music in this Book

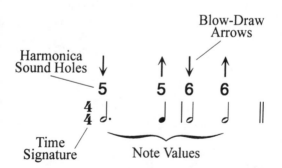

Blow-Draw Arrows

Harmonica Sound Holes

Time Signature

Note Values

A Child of the King

Little Maggie

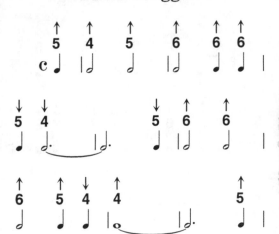

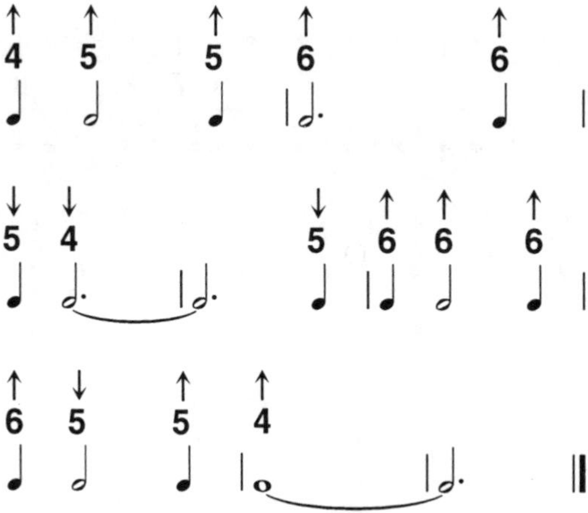
4 5 5 6 6
5 4 5 6 6 6
6 5 5 4

Rovin' Gambler

Careless Love

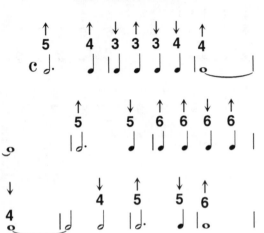

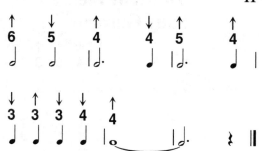

Down by the Sally Gardens

14 Wraggle-Taggle Gypsies

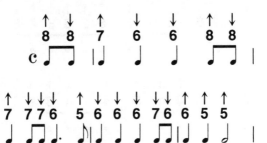

Sometimes I Feel like a Motherless Child

↑ ↑ ↑ ↑ ↑ ↓ ↑ ↓ ↑   ↓
7 8 7 8 7 8 8 8 7   6

↑ ↓ ↑ ↓ ↑ ↓ ↑ ↓ ↑   ↓
7 8 7 8 7 8 8 8 7   6

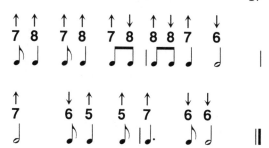

Billy Boy

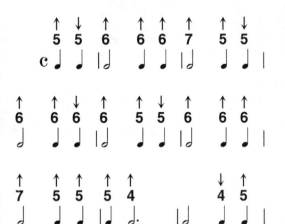

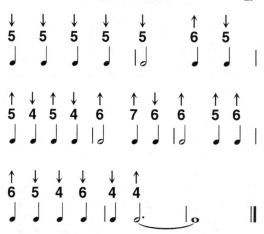

Blind Mary

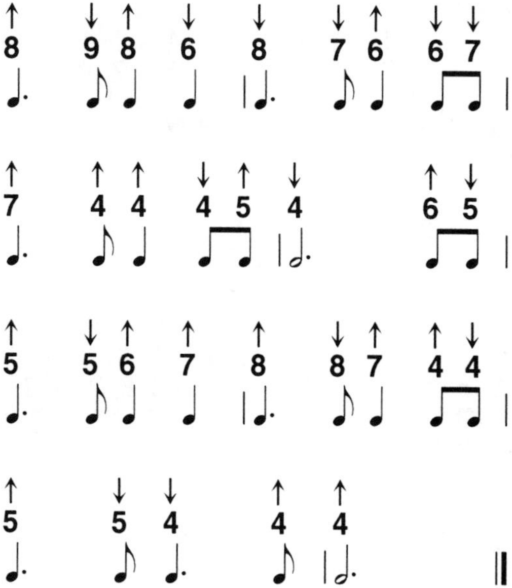
↑8 ↓9 ↑8 ↓6 ↓8 ↓7 ↑6 ↓6 ↓7
↑7 ↑4 ↑4 ↓4 ↑5 ↓4 ↑6 ↓5
↑5 ↓5 ↑6 ↑7 ↑8 ↓8 ↑7 ↑4 ↓4
↑5 ↓5 ↓4 ↑4 ↑4

Heaven, Heaven

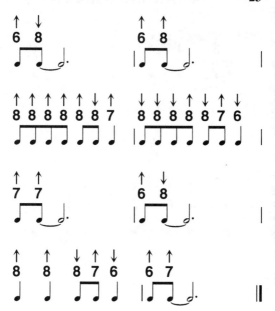

Cockles and Mussels

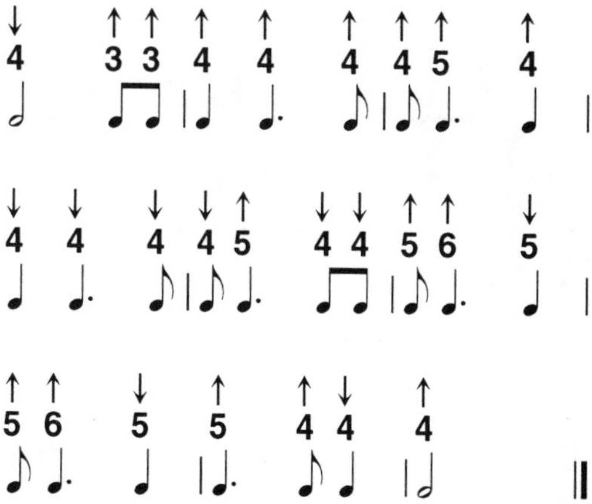
4 3 3 4 4 4 4 5 4
4 4 4 4 5 4 4 5 6 5
5 6 5 5 4 4 4

Red River Valley

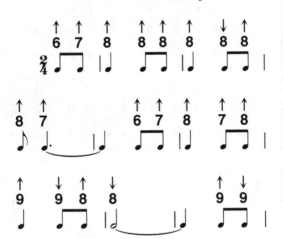

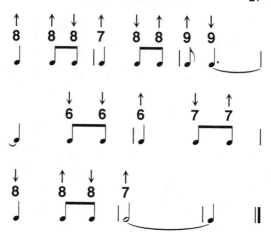

Rise & Shine

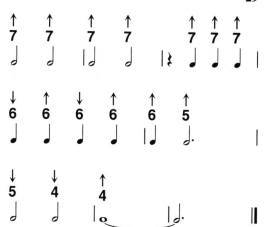

Rock of Ages

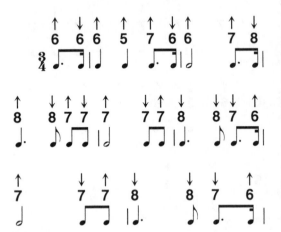

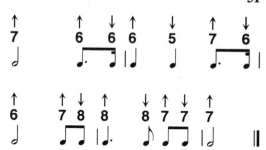

Silent Night

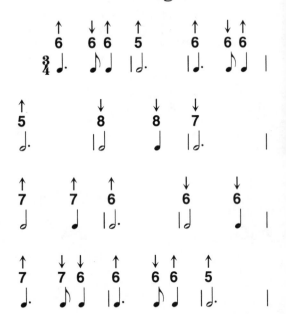

I am a Pilgrim

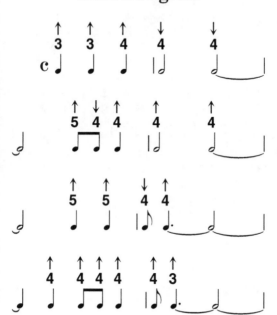

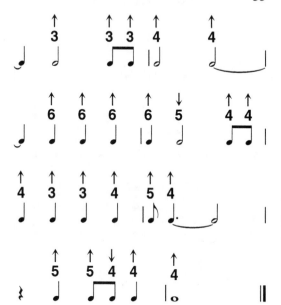

Roll On Buddy

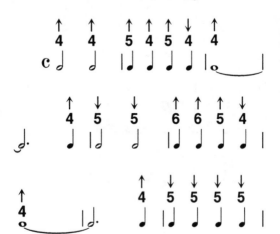

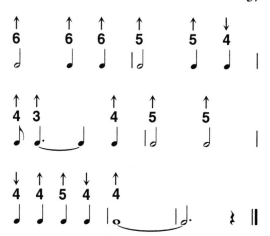

Hand Me Down my Walking Cane

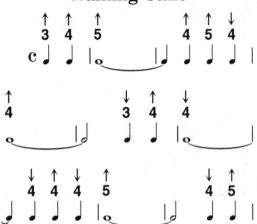

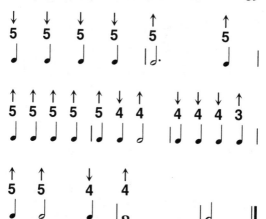

I Feel like Traveling On

What Shall we Do with the Drunken Sailor?

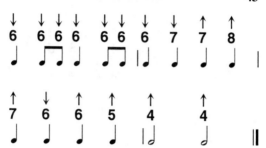

America

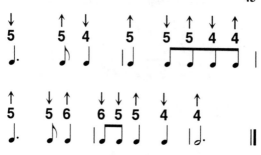

The Foggy, Foggy Dew

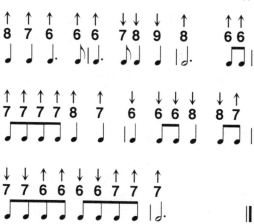

Swing Low,
Sweet Chariot

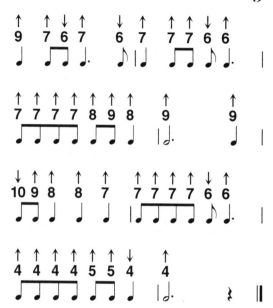

Wondrous Love

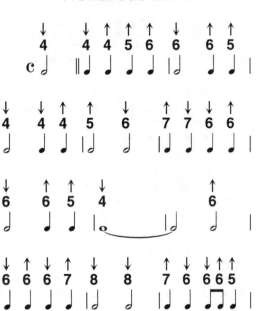

John Henry

↑ ↓ ↑ ↑ ↑ ↓ ↑ ↓ ↑   ↑ ↓
6 6 7 7 7 6 6 6 7   6 6

↑   ↑   ↑ ↓ ↑ ↑ ↑   ↑ ↓
7   7   7 6 6 5 6   6 6

↑ ↑ ↑ ↓ ↑   ↑   ↓   ↑   ↑
7 7 7 6 6   5   6   5   4

Year of Jubilo

Alabama Bound

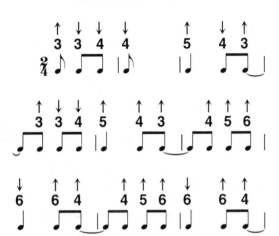

Wildwood Flower

↑ ↓ ↑   ↓ ↑ ↑   ↓ ↑
5 5 6   6 7 5   5 5
c ♩ ♩ |𝅗𝅥   ♩ ♩ |𝅗𝅥   ♩ ♩ |

↓ ↑ ↓ ↑   ↑ ↓ ↑   ↑ ↑
4 5 4 4   5 5 6   6 7
𝅗𝅥 ♩ ♩ |𝅗𝅥   ♩ ♩ |𝅗𝅥   ♩ ♩ |

↑ ↓ ↑ ↓   ↑ ↓ ↑   ↑
5 5 5 4   5 4 4   6
𝅗𝅥 ♩ ♩ |𝅗𝅥   ♩ ♩ |𝅗𝅥   𝄽 ♩ |

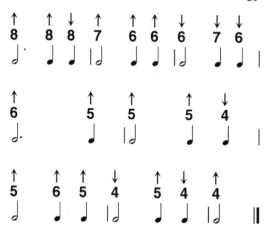

Liza Jane

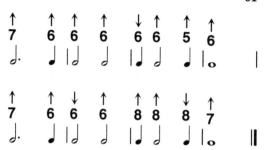

62   There's a River of Life

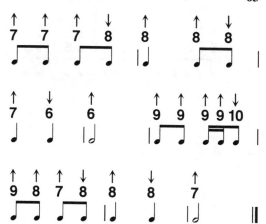

64   Rock-a-My Soul

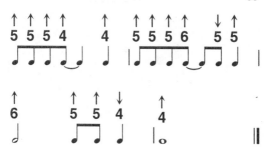

In the Pines

↑	↓	↓	↑	↑
5	6	6	8	8

↓	↑	↓	↓ ↓	↑	↑ ↑
8	7	6	6 6	8	8 8

↓	↑	↓	↑
8	7	6	5

↓	↓ ↓	↑	↑ ↑	↓	↓ ↑
6	6 6	8	8 8	8	8 7

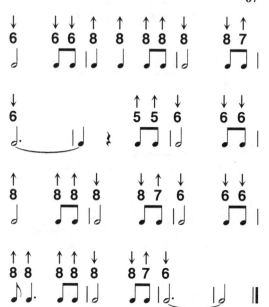

The Gal I
Left Behind Me

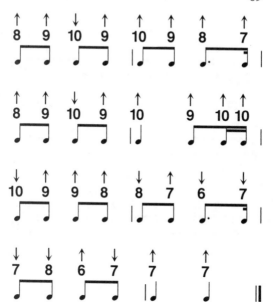

70

Oh, Susanna

Crawdad Song

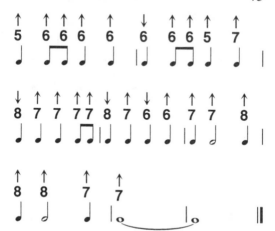

My Home's Across the Smoky Mountains

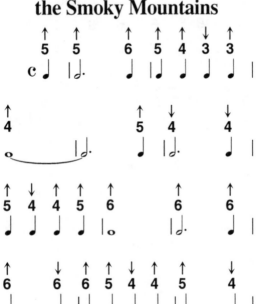

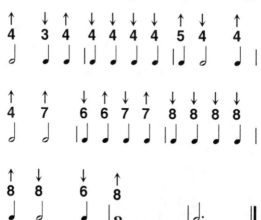

Ring, Ring the Banjo

↑ ↑ ↑ ↑ ↓ ↑ ↑ ↑ ↑
6 6 5 4 4 5 6 6 6

↓ ↑ ↑ ↑ ↓ ↓ ↑ ↓ ↑ ↓
6 6 5 4 4 4 4 4 5 5

↑ ↑ ↓ ↓ ↑ ↓ ↓ ↑ ↑
6 7 6 6 6 5 4 4 4 6

↑ ↑ ↑ ↓ ↑ ↑ ↑ ↑ ↓ ↑ ↑ ↑
6 5 4 4 5 6 6 6 6 6 5 4

78 Bringing in the Sheaves

Lolly Too Dum

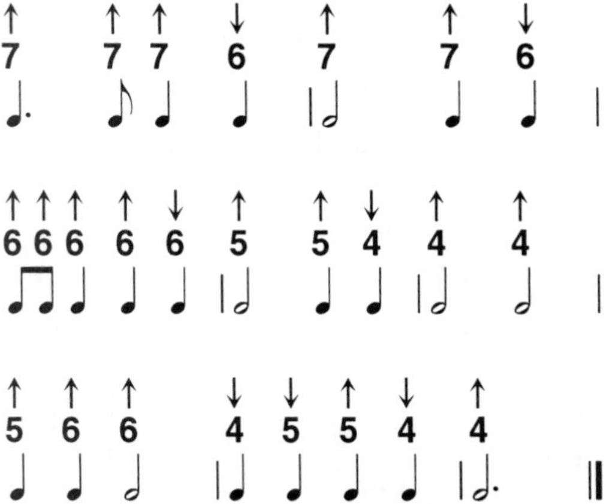
↑ ↑ ↑ ↓ ↑ ↑ ↓
7 7 7 6 7 7 6
↑ ↑ ↑ ↑ ↓ ↑ ↑ ↓ ↑ ↑
6 6 6 6 6 5 5 4 4 4
↑ ↑ ↑ ↓ ↓ ↑ ↓ ↑
5 6 6 4 5 5 4 4

Hard, Ain't it Hard

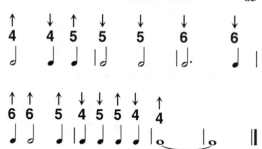

Camptown Races

↑ ↑ ↑ ↑ ↑ ↓ ↑ ↑
6 6 6 5 6 6 6 5

↑ ↓ ↑ ↓ ↑ ↑ ↑ ↑ ↑
5 4 5 4 6 6 6 5 6

↓ ↑ ↑ ↓ ↑ ↓ ↑
6 6 5 4 5 4 4

Si Beag Si Mór

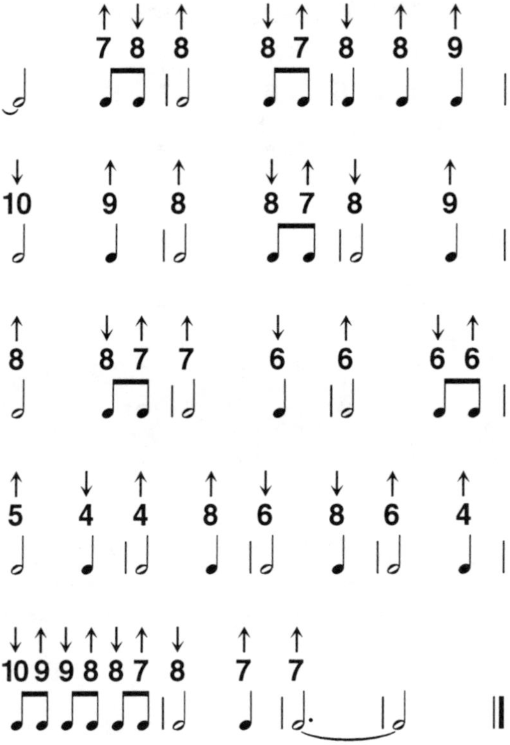
↑ ↓ ↑ ↓ ↑ ↓ ↑ ↑
7 8 8 8 7 8 8 9
↓ ↑ ↑ ↓ ↑ ↓ ↑
10 9 8 8 7 8 9
↑ ↓ ↑ ↑ ↓ ↑ ↓ ↑
8 8 7 7 6 6 6 6
↑ ↓ ↑ ↑ ↓ ↓ ↑ ↑
5 4 4 8 6 8 6 4
↓ ↑ ↓ ↑ ↓ ↑ ↓ ↑ ↑
10 9 9 8 8 7 8 7 7

I Will Sing
the Wondrous Story

Angelina Baker

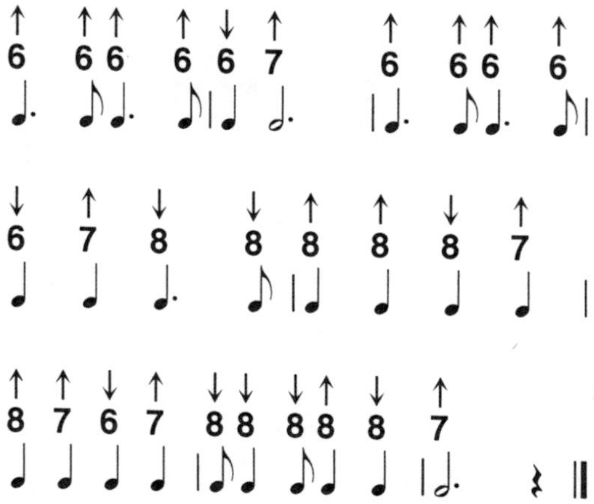

New River Train

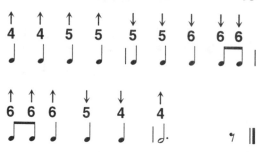

East Virginia

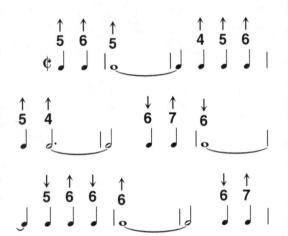

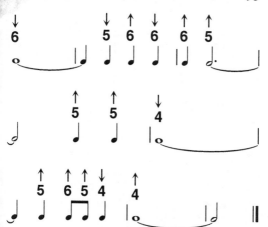

Hey Ho, Nobody Home